MY FIRST STEPS
on the
Covenant Path

For my children, Henry, Betsy, and Max.

ISBN 13: 978-1-4621-4812-7

Published by CFI, an imprint of Cedar Fort, Inc.
2373 W. 700 S., Suite 100, Springville, UT 84663
Distributed by Cedar Fort, Inc., www.cedarfort.com

Library of Congress Control Number: 2024944589

Cover and interior layout by Shawnda T. Craig
Cover design © 2024 Cedar Fort, Inc.

Printed in China

10 9 8 7 6 5 4 3 2 1

Printed on acid-free paper

MY FIRST STEPS
on the
Covenant Path

Cari Thompson

CFI • An Imprint of Cedar Fort, Inc.
Springville, Utah

Hi! I'm Elizabeth,
but everyone calls me Betsy.

I'm eight years old, and I just took my first steps on the COVENANT PATH.

What does COVENANT PATH mean?

"COVENANT" means a sacred, two-way promise between YOU and HEAVENLY FATHER.

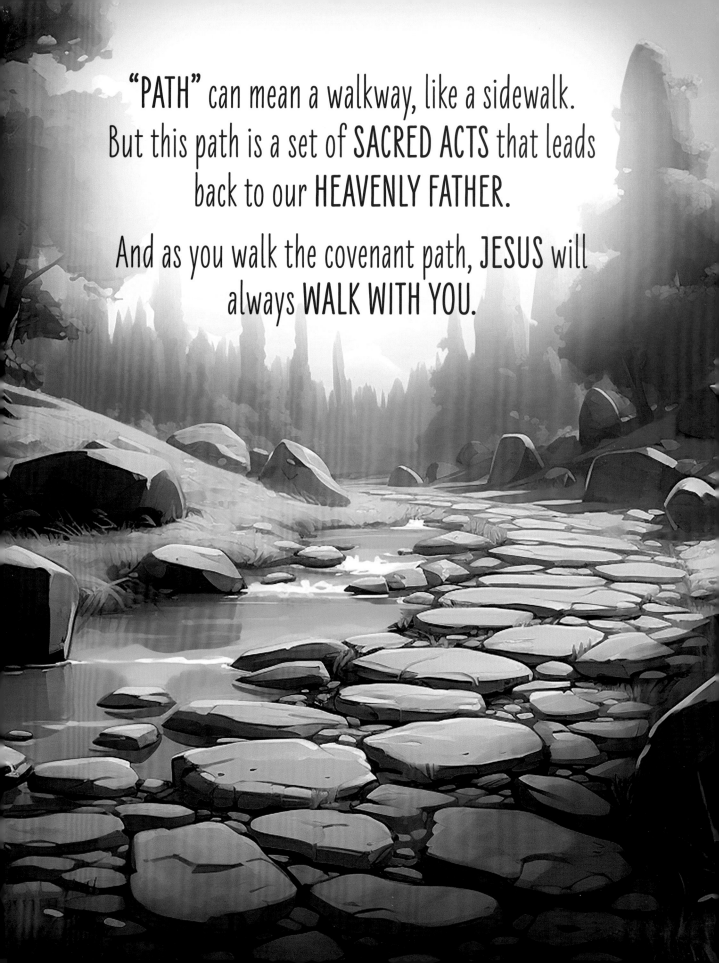

"PATH" can mean a walkway, like a sidewalk. But this path is a set of SACRED ACTS that leads back to our HEAVENLY FATHER.

And as you walk the covenant path, JESUS will always WALK WITH YOU.

So far, I've made three covenants with Heavenly Father . . .

I've been **BAPTIZED**, received the **GIFT OF THE HOLY GHOST**, and taken the **SACRAMENT.**

START

BAPTISM

The FIRST STEP on the covenant path

BAPTISMAL COVENANTS

When I was baptized, I **PROMISED**
Heavenly Father I would ...

1

**Take Jesus Christ's
name upon me**

I will be a
missionary and help
with His work.

2

**Keep His
commandments**

I will try to keep
my thoughts, language,
and actions pure.

3

**Serve Him
to the end**

I will serve the
people around me.

Heavenly Father **PROMISED** me He would ...

1

Give me the Gift of the Holy Ghost
He comforts me and helps me make good choices.

2

Forgive me when I repent
He gives me a fresh start.

3

Love me forever
His love is infinite and perfect.

My baptism day was the BEST!
I was so HAPPY, because I knew I was doing what
HEAVENLY FATHER wanted me to do.

I know Heavenly Father was **HAPPY WITH ME**, because He was **HAPPY WITH JESUS** when Jesus was baptized.

"And lo a voice from heaven, saying, This is my beloved Son, in whom I am **WELL PLEASED**."

When JESUS WAS BAPTIZED, He was obeying Heavenly Father's COMMANDMENTS.

When I was baptized, I was KEEPING THE COMMANDMENTS and FOLLOWING JESUS CHRIST'S EXAMPLE.

GIFT of the
HOLY GHOST

Our CONSTANT COMPANION and FRIEND

After I was baptized, I was given the
GIFT OF THE HOLY GHOST.

When you receive the gift of the Holy Ghost, you get to learn how the **SPIRIT SPEAKS TO YOU.** The more you practice listening to the Spirit, the better you'll get at it!

Why is it called the **GIFT** of the Holy Ghost?

When you get a **PRESENT,** do you leave it in the wrapping? No way!

You rip it open and **ENJOY YOUR GIFT.**

The **GIFT OF THE HOLY GHOST** works the same way.

You have to open your present
(ask the Holy Ghost to be with you),
and enjoy your gift
(listen to and follow the spirit).

When you RECEIVE THE GIFT of the Holy Ghost, you are BLESSED with ...

happiness

comfort

guidance

understanding

inspiration

truth

protection

faith in CHRIST

The HOLY GHOST is the BEST GIFT EVER!

the SACRAMENT

REMEMBER and RENEW baptismal covenants

The day after my baptism and confirmation,
I was able to take my **NEXT STEP** on the **COVENANT PATH:**
Taking the **SACRAMENT.**

Before my baptism, I took the **BREAD** and **WATER** lots of times.

But now that I'm baptized, it means something more.
Now, **I RENEW MY BAPTISMAL COVENANTS** each time
I take the sacrament.

"Renew" means to make something NEW, FRESH, or STRONG again.

So, every time I take the sacrament, I MAKE PROMISES to Heavenly Father again, and HE MAKES PROMISES to me again.

It's like I'm getting BAPTIZED EVERY WEEK!

my NEXT STEPS on the COVENANT PATH

TEMPLE and PRIESTHOOD blessings

The year I turn 12, I'll be able to go inside the TEMPLE and BE BAPTIZED for people who died before learning about the gospel.

BAPTISMS for the DEAD

The year boys turn 12, they can be ORDAINED to the PRIESTHOOD and start SERVING in their wards and families.

PRIESTHOOD SERVICE

And when I'm ready, I can go through the temple for myself to make **MORE PROMISES** and receive **MORE BLESSINGS** from **HEAVENLY FATHER.**

TEMPLE ENDOWMENT

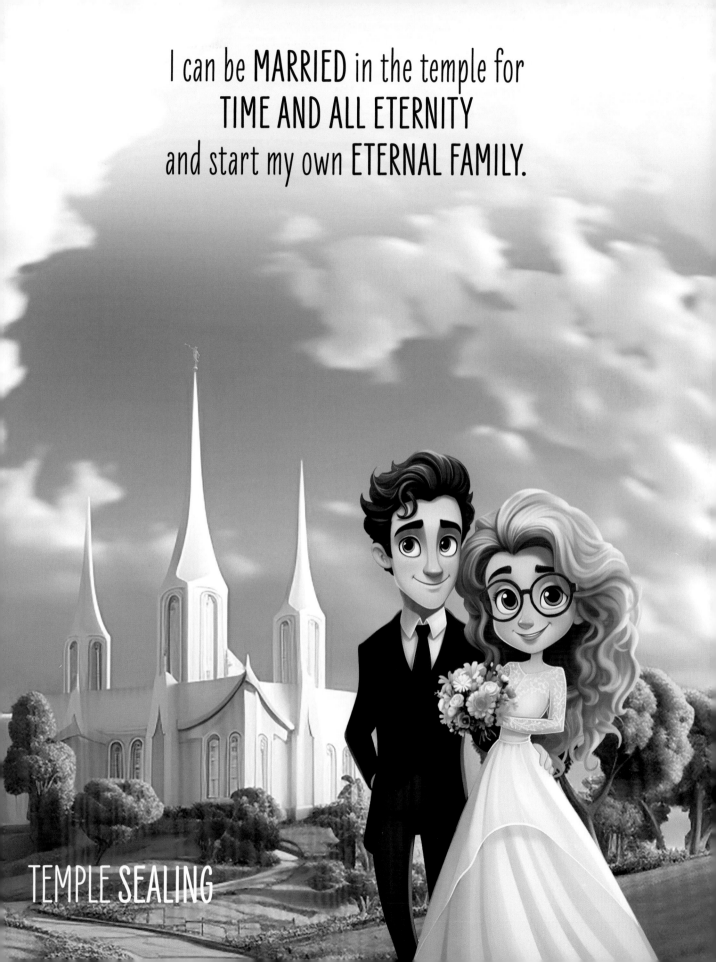

As I stay on the **COVENANT PATH** and continue to make and keep **SACRED COVENANTS,** Jesus will always **WALK WITH ME.**

Because He **LOVES ME,** He wants me to **BE HAPPY,** and He wants me to **RETURN TO HIM.**

Scripture References

BAPTISMAL COVENANTS
Mosiah 2:17

BLESSINGS
Galatians 5:22; Luke 12:12;
Doctrine & Covenants 36:2;
Doctrine & Covenants 6:15;
2 Nephi 32:5; Moroni 10:5;
Doctrine & Covenants 46:13

WELL PLEASED
Matthew 3:17

the SACRAMENT
Luke 22:19-20
3 Nephi 18:10

JESUS' BAPTISM
2 Nephi 9:23; Matthew 3: 13-17;
3 Nephi 18:16

BAPTISMS for the DEAD
1 Corinthians 15:29
1 Peter 4:6

GIFT of the HOLY GHOST
Doctrine & Covenants 88:33
Doctrine & Covenants 8:2

TEMPLE COVENANTS
Doctrine & Covenants 14:7
Doctrine & Covenants 109:22